WHERE DO I LIVE?
PROVINCE

A Crabtree Roots Book

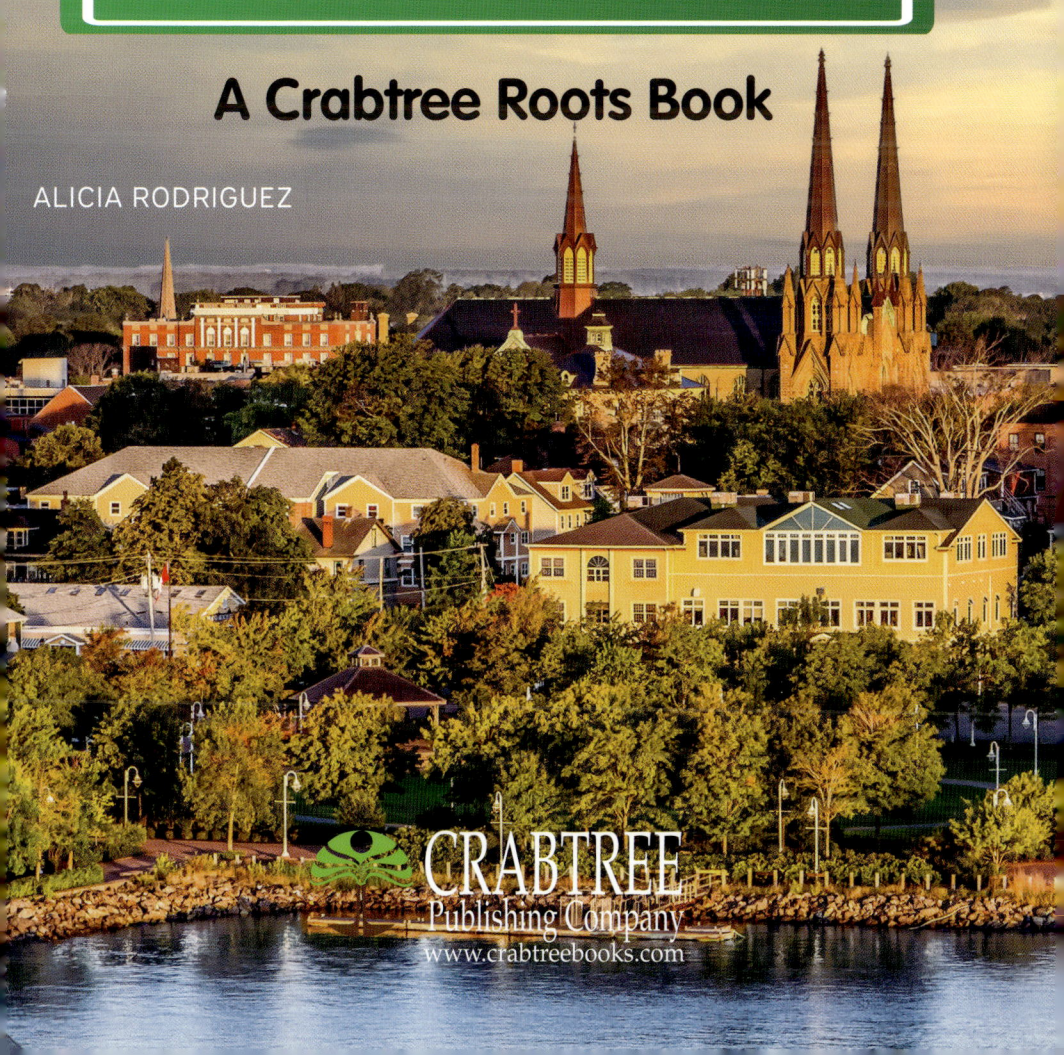

ALICIA RODRIGUEZ

School-to-Home Support for Caregivers and Teachers

This book helps children grow by letting them practice reading. Here are a few guiding questions to help the reader with building his or her comprehension skills. Possible answers appear here in red.

Before Reading:
- What do I think this book is about?
    - *I think this book is about what a province looks like.*
    - *I think this book is about what you can find in a province.*
- What do I want to learn about this topic?
    - *I want to learn how big a province is.*
    - *I want to learn who runs a province.*

During Reading:
- I wonder why...
    - *I wonder why a province has its own flag.*
    - *I wonder why a country can be made up of provinces.*
- What have I learned so far?
    - *I have learned that the premier is the leader of a province.*
    - *I have learned that some provinces have beaches.*

After Reading:
- What details did I learn about this topic?
    - *I have learned that provinces can be different shapes and sizes.*
    - *I have learned that provinces have leaders.*
- Read the book again and look for the vocabulary words.
    - *I see the word **province** on page 3 and the word **flags** on page 12. The other vocabulary words are found on page 14.*

I live in a **province**.

3

It is part of a **country**.

CANADA

- Yukon
- Northwest Territories
- Nunavut
- British Columbia
- Alberta
- Saskatchewan
- Manitoba
- Ontario
- Quebec
- Newfoundland and Labrador
- New Brunswick
- Prince Edward Island
- Nova Scotia

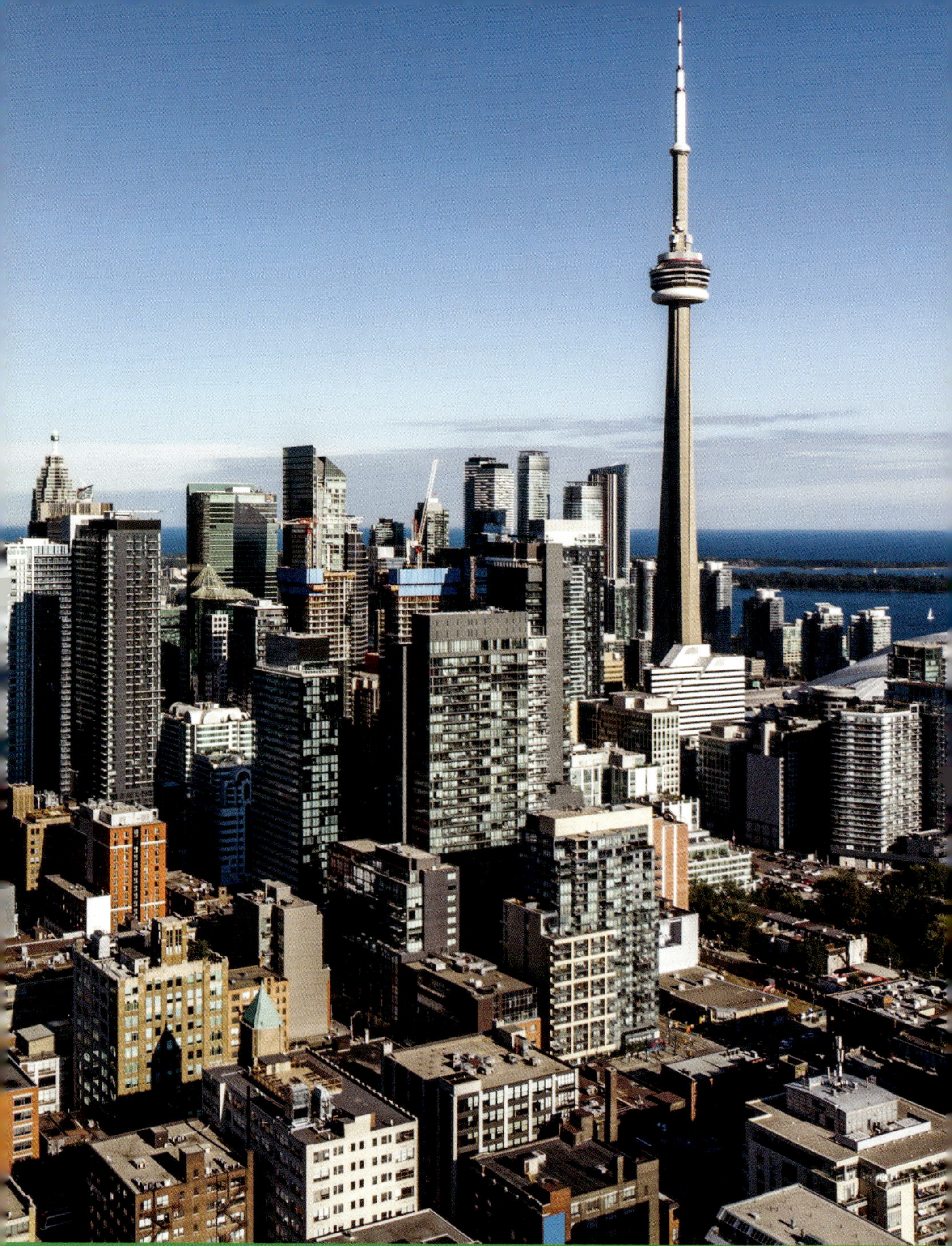

Each province has a **capital city**.

The **premier** is the leader.

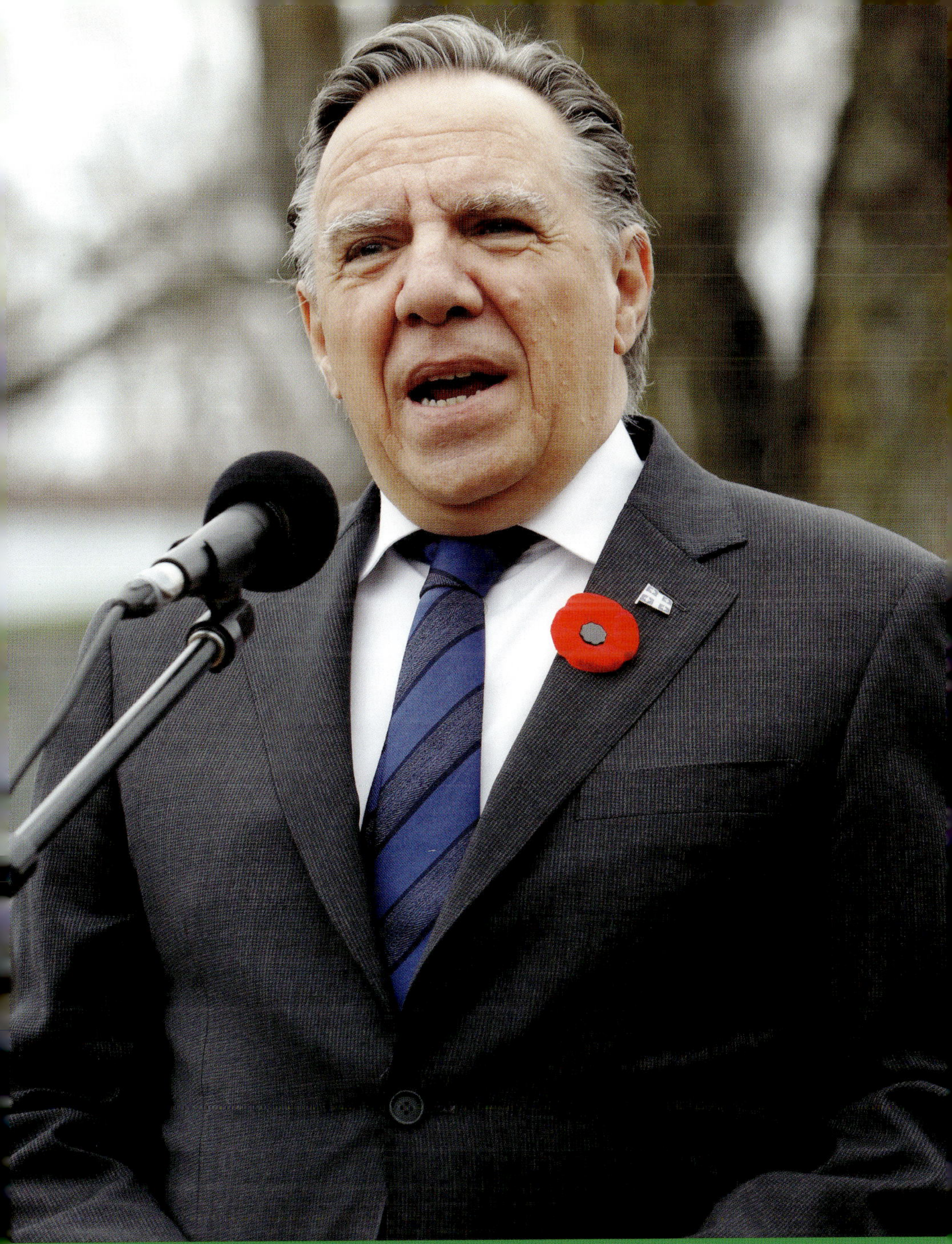

Some provinces have **beaches**.

Some provinces have **mountains**.

All provinces have **flags**.

13

Word List
Sight Words

a	I	of
all	in	some
each	is	the
has	it	
have	live	

Words to Know

beaches

capital city

country

flags

mountains

premier

province

14

34 Words

I live in a **province**.

It is part of a **country**.

Each province has a **capital city**.

The **premier** is the leader.

Some provinces have **beaches**.

Some provinces have **mountains**.

All provinces have **flags**.

CRABTREE
Publishing Company

Written by: Alicia Rodriguez
Designed by: Rhea Wallace
Series Development: James Earley
Proofreader: Janine Deschenes
Educational Consultant: Marie Lemke M.Ed.

Photographs:
Shutterstock: R.M. Nunes: cover; Darryl Brooks: p. 1;
 Firefighter Montreal: p. 3, 14; boreala: p. 5, 14; Jeff
 Whyte: p. 6, 13, 14; Voinau Pavel: p. 9, 14; EB Adventure
 Photography: p. 10, 14; Pavel Tvrdy: p. 11, 14

Library and Archives Canada Cataloguing in Publication

Title: Province / Alicia Rodriguez.
Names: Rodriguez, Alicia (Children's author), author.
Description: Series statement: Where do I live? |
 "A Crabtree roots book".
Identifiers: Canadiana (print) 20210182938 |
 Canadiana (ebook) 20210182946 |
 ISBN 9781427160003 (hardcover) |
 ISBN 9781427160065 (softcover) |
 ISBN 9781427133601 (HTML) |
 ISBN 9781427134202 (EPUB) |
 ISBN 9781427160249 (read-along ebook)
Subjects: LCSH: Canadian provinces—Juvenile literature.
Classification: LCC FC58 .R64 2022 | DDC j971—dc23

Library of Congress Cataloging-in-Publication Data

Available at the Library of Congress

Crabtree Publishing Company
www.crabtreebooks.com   1-800-387-7650

Printed in the U.S.A./062021/CG20210401

Copyright © 2022 **CRABTREE PUBLISHING COMPANY**

All rights reserved. No part of this publication may be reproduced, stored in a retrieval system or be transmitted in any form or by any means, electronic, mechanical, photocopying, recording, or otherwise, without the prior written permission of Crabtree Publishing Company. In Canada: We acknowledge the financial support of the Government of Canada through the Canada Book Fund for our publishing activities.

Published in the United States
Crabtree Publishing
347 Fifth Avenue, Suite 1402-145
New York, NY, 10016

Published in Canada
Crabtree Publishing
616 Welland Ave.
St. Catharines, Ontario L2M 5V6